PRAISE FOR
THE INTELLIGENT WORK BOOK

"Visual + verbal = inspirational."

Chris Barez-Brown, Founder, Upping Your Elvis,
and author, *Wake Up! Escaping A Life On Autopilot*

**"One thing remains constant with all of Kevin's books
– practical advice that makes us better.
The Intelligent Work Book is no exception."**

Richard Morris, CEO UK and President EMEA, Initiative

**"Duncan says your audience remembers 70% of your
beginning, 20% of your middle and 100% of the end.
Let me end with this: BRILLIANT!"**

Marty Neumeier, author, *Scramble: A business thriller*

**"It is rare to find a book that makes you stop and
think about how you think. Simple visual wisdom from
Kevin Duncan which is well worth a look."**

Helen Calcraft, Founding Partner, Lucky Generals

FOR OTHER TITLES
IN THE SERIES...

CONCISE
ADVICE
LAB

SMALL BOOKS: BIG IDEAS

CLEVER CONTENT, DYNAMIC IDEAS, PRACTICAL
SOLUTIONS AND ENGAGING VISUALS –
A CATALYST TO INSPIRE NEW WAYS OF THINKING
AND PROBLEM-SOLVING IN A COMPLEX WORLD

conciseadvicelab.com

Published by
LID Publishing
An imprint of LID Business Media Ltd.
LABS House, 15-19 Bloomsbury Way,
London, WC1A 2TH, UK

info@lidpublishing.com
www.lidpublishing.com

A member of:

businesspublishersroundtable.com

© Kevin Duncan, 2020
© LID Publishing Limited, 2020
Reprinted in 2022

Printed by Imak Ofset

ISBN: 978-1-912555-70-3

Cover and page design: Caroline Li

THE INTELLIGENT WORK BOOK

A VISUAL GUIDE TO SORTING OUT LIFE AND WORK

KEVIN DUNCAN

MADRID | MEXICO CITY | LONDON
BUENOS AIRES | BOGOTA | SHANGHAI

CONTENTS

PART SEVEN: SELLING

PART EIGHT: NEGOTIATING

INTRODUCTION

Seven years ago I noticed that many of my attendees in training were taking notes in a new way – drawing shapes instead of writing old-fashioned longhand lecture notes.

So I wondered how many diagrams there were in my training materials. The answer was 46, so I added four more and wrote *The Diagrams Book*.

I had no idea at the time that there was an entire world market in visual thinking. Over time I seem to have become "the diagrams guy."

Editions of the book have now come in from Japan, Taiwan, Korea, Germany, France, Spain, the Netherlands, Sweden, China, Poland and Hungary, and there is more to come from Russia and Thailand.

All over the world, it is clear that many find it hard to express themselves and solve problems purely with words. Diagrams and visuals are superb for organizing your thinking in so many ways.

My next challenge was to try to combine the two. Would it be possible to interweave narrative and visuals to create a guide to sorting stuff out? This is my attempt to do just that: *The Intelligent Work Book*.

In my opinion, balanced intelligence comes from combining the power of the visual and the verbal, and the result becomes a practical workbook that anyone can use. From thinking, doing, working, planning and prioritizing, through to presenting, selling, negotiating, progressing in your career or just joking around, it's all covered here.

It can be done, so here's to intelligent work.

Good luck, and keep me posted on how you get on.

Kevin Duncan
Westminster, 2020

A WORD ON THINKING

Too many people blunder straight into doing things
before they have thought them through properly.

Thinking is free and we should all do it more often.

It pays to ponder before you take action.

Start by working out your style, and consider how you
come across at home and in work. It is important to be
yourself wherever you are.

Develop a knack for addressing the issues head on,
and not burying the tough stuff or pretending it isn't there.
That will always come back to haunt you.

Think about motivation and how it affects the energy and
effort that goes into the things that you feel matter most.

Adopt the ability both to look at the big picture and
be able to look at detail. Too much of one or the other
leads to an imbalanced approach.

And don't be fooled by dead ends masquerading
as opportunities.

As Barbara Castle once said: "Think, think, think again.
It will hurt at first, but you'll get used to it."

PART ONE

THINKING

1. PERSONALITY
WORK YOU VS NORMAL YOU

Some people behave quite differently at work than they do in their personal lives. This may be okay, but it can also lead to stress. A person who is totally different in each context has a life that looks like this:

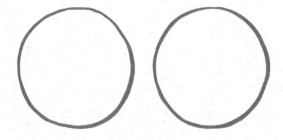

In extreme cases, this is almost like having two different personalities, or a split one. Those who feel and behave this way spend a lot of time watching what they say and do at work, and most people find this draining and stressful. So the big question is: how much common ground is there between your personal and business life?

Look at the two diagrams at the top of the opposite page. If it looks like the diagram on the left, there is probably a fair bit of tension in deciding how to 'behave' appropriately at work. Those who struggle with this often call it *covering* – covering up certain behavioural traits in the interests of fitting in. The diagram on the right shows some overlap, but is it enough?

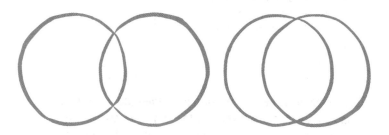

Arguably the happiest person looks like this:

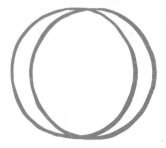

They are happy to be themselves at work, and as such there is no tension and no need to pretend.

 THIS WORKS
Being yourself at work.

 THIS DOESN'T
Pretending to be who you're not.

2. ATTITUDE
THREE GOOD, THREE BAD

This technique is helpful for solving complex problems with many variables, such as which strategy to choose, which markets to pursue or which components to concentrate on in a project.
To start, everyone involved writes down the three best things about the topic and the three worst.

This must be done without conferring so that responses are unbiased. All the results are collected and collated into two new lists of good and bad. If ten people do this, in theory this could generate a list of 30 good and 30 bad, but in practice there are rarely more than six or seven points on each side. This shows what degree of consensus there is. If the good outweigh the bad, it will look something like this:

This is good news because it means there is plenty of good stuff, and the bad can either be dealt with or ignored. However, if the bad outweigh the good, it will look like this:

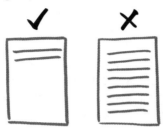

At first glance, this appears depressing, but it doesn't have to be. If dealing with a project, the issues on the right either confirm that the project should not go ahead, or they provide an immediate checklist of everything that needs to be rectified before proceeding. If dealing with a brief, the bad list will almost certainly contain a vital deficiency or issue that needs to be addressed. Once identified, this becomes the epicentre of the task – the purpose or objective to be tackled head on.

This technique is guaranteed to promote honesty and clarity at the start of any project.

 THIS WORKS
Confronting bad things at the start.

 THIS DOESN'T
Pretending that bad stuff isn't there.

3. ENTHUSIASM
MOTIVATIONAL DIPS

At the beginning of any project or relationship (business or personal), everyone is very excited. Energy and commitment are high, and so is enthusiasm. It's an upward trajectory.

As time progresses, there is always a dip in motivation. It doesn't matter whether this is a one-week project or a three-year relationship, there always is.

When this happens, it is vital to get into a phase of learning and understanding, and to do it fast. This is the only way to redeem waning motivation.

Sometimes this phase takes a long time, but it's worth it. Investment of time and effort here pays dividends. If an individual or company has reached this stage, then they can recognize it for what it is and take appropriate measures. If it is a relationship, then both parties should discuss the dip and talk through the benefits of learning and understanding.

A mature approach to this should lead to renewed vigour and a successful relationship over time or conclusion to a project. If not, failure or a relationship split may be the outcome.

In almost every instance this kind of thinking should enable any company or individual to predict when a motivational dip is likely to occur. Rather than being pessimistic, this enables any party to anticipate the moment, discuss it and take action to remedy the situation before it becomes terminal.

THIS WORKS
Anticipating the motivational dip.

THIS DOESN'T
Assuming motivation will stay high.

4. PERSPECTIVES
ZOOM IN, ZOOM OUT

Modern business comes with a built-in dilemma: how to cope with the big picture and the detail at the same time. This is an issue that vexes business leaders. On the one hand they are concerned with the overall strategic direction of a company and, on the other, they are perpetually dragged into specific operational detail.

The knack is to be able to zoom in and zoom out fast, all day, every day. Zooming out reveals the big picture, and zooming in shows the detail. The first is all about widening options and attaining distance. The second is all about understanding the true operational or technical detail.

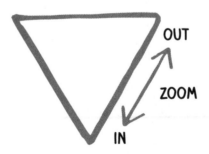

There are dangers on both sides of this dilemma. Those who consistently talk about strategy (the big picture) are often accused of generalizing too much, and failing to understand the detail. Those who zoom in too much are often seen as micromanaging or being too down in the weeds. A flexible balance is needed.

This is why T-shaped executives are so highly valued. The crossbar of the T demonstrates their broad understanding of a business, and the vertical shows their deep specific knowledge.

And in multi-faceted businesses, a successful manager may have to become adept on many fronts – a series of Ts in a row, with a profile more like a fine-toothed comb.

THIS WORKS
Constantly reviewing both big and small issues.

THIS DOESN'T
Only thinking big, or only concentrating on detail.

5. CLARITY
DIRECTIONAL PERSPECTIVES

Thinking about markets and business often leads to erroneous strategic thinking, whereby people are convinced there is some kind of opportunity when in fact there isn't. It all starts with a market map, plotting a couple of the most important variables affecting it, usually on an X/Y grid like this:

Typically, this is then populated with a number of products, companies, brands, competitors, audiences, or whatever is being discussed. Sometimes this leads to a very helpful map showing clear distinctions that can then be discussed and analyzed. In the example on the left, if the vertical axis is premium/cheap and the horizontal well-known/unknown, we can see that the product on its own top right is the most premium and well-known in relation to those in the other quadrants.

On other occasions, the market is so crowded and confused that the resulting map is a mess – perhaps something like this:

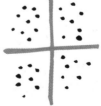

This is a picture of a crowded and confused market. Arguably the most deceptive type of market map looks like this:

This yields an entire quadrant that appears to be unoccupied by any product or brand. Wise strategists call this fool's gold white space. It makes it appear as though there is a gap in the market, but is there a market in the gap? At this point, everyone concerned should ask: what does someone else know that we don't? There may be a very good reason to avoid this area. Most likely, taking new perspectives in this way will generate a construct like this:

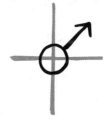

This shows a desired direction of travel from a current state of affairs towards a new market position – effectively an entire strategy on one chart. That's something we can all understand.

THIS WORKS
Looking at complete topics.

THIS DOESN'T
Being fooled by false opportunities.

THINKING SUMMARY

THIS WORKS
- Being yourself at work
- Confronting bad things at the start
- Anticipating the motivational dip
- Constantly reviewing both big and small issues
- Looking at complete topics

THIS DOESN'T
- Pretending to be who you're not
- Pretending that bad stuff isn't there
- Assuming motivation will stay high
- Only thinking big, or only concentrating on detail
- Being fooled by false opportunities

DRAW YOUR THOUGHTS HERE

A WORD ON PLANNING

Everybody seems to love planning, but a plan is just that
– a plan. Just because we are all staring at an apparently
marvellous plan, it doesn't mean that things are
actually going to happen like that.

So we need to accept that things change, or will not
come to pass, and think harder about alternatives
– plans B, C and more.

The year never works out how you think, but you can almost
always predict when things will go wrong, as they always do.

You can then anticipate difficulties and cope with
them better.

Procrastination doesn't work. If you are going to panic,
then do it early. It's called precrastination.

Don't fixate on the deadline. Instead, concentrate on what
I call the liveline – the actual work that needs doing now.

Now is when you affect the future, so be clinical about what
you are focusing on, and aim for the bullseye every time.
Clarity wins, with a healthy dose of flexibility in reserve.

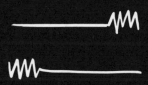

PART TWO

PLANNING

1. DECEPTION
FICTIONAL PLANS

Businesses love to plan, and there is nothing particularly wrong with that. However, the problems begin when people start believing the plan. Some companies spend months planning, and eventually they will produce a year plan that looks something like this:

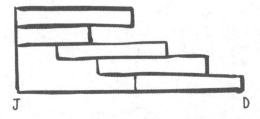

J   D

Everyone gets very excited because the plan looks authoritative and is beautifully art directed. Everybody nods and walks out of the room under the impression that what is written on the plan is exactly what will happen. But it won't. So a more realistic depiction of the plan might look something like this:

If that's true, then a more iterative approach might be more honest and, ultimately, more successful. In other words, don't allow the apparent authority of the beautifully crafted plan to convince you

or the team that success is assured. Plan B is often better than plan A, and accepting this possibility before everyone is emotionally and financially committed to plan A could save a lot of heartache. In which case, the plan may look like this:

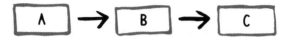

This is similar to iterative planning, but with a twist. In this version, the possibility of plans B and C are already built in to the strategic and planning process – not simply dreamt up at speed when plan A has not worked. This type of thinking reduces surprises. Part of this philosophy is an acknowledgement that most projects have a fuzzy front end. This is a period in which uncertainty should be expected and embraced, before clarity emerges. This model suggests a pattern such as this:

It looks more uncertain, but it does get there eventually.

THIS WORKS
Assuming the plan won't happen.

THIS DOESN'T
Assuming the plan will happen.

2. PACING
THE YEAR THAT NEVER IS

Realistic and sensible planning can be extended beyond projects and strategies to look at a company's entire plan for the year. The problem with most year plans is that they have fiction built in. In other words, senior executives are pushing for growth, but they don't necessarily know where it is coming from. Those writing the plan tend to be told, for example, that 10% growth is mandatory, so a plan is produced like this:

The dotted line verifies that this year's performance will be better than it was last year, but this is often wishful thinking, and probably won't happen like that. Instead, if we view the solid line as average performance and the dotted line as real performance, a company's efforts over a year will most likely have highs and lows, like this:

If that is a more realistic prediction, then experienced practitioners who know the business well should be able to anticipate the true pattern of the year in a reasonably accurate way. In this example, the business will overperform in March, May and the autumn, but will underperform in January, April, the summer and Christmas. This shape broadly reflects annual holidays and peaks and troughs of staff enthusiasm. Suddenly, the year looks like this:

If they are prepared to acknowledge these ups and downs, enlightened CEOs, finance directors and planners can then overlay the plan with decision windows, crisis moments and anticipated income, to generate a truly well-informed plan.

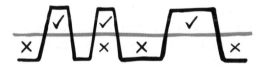

The ticks in the peaks anticipate decision-making and decisive action. The crosses anticipate crises of underperformance or lack of investment and resourcing. Now the true picture of the year becomes clearer.

THIS WORKS
Anticipating work fluctuations.

THIS DOESN'T
Assuming even effort across the year.

3. TIMING
PROCRASTINATION AND PANICKING

Most students put off everything until the last minute. This type of procrastination almost always leads to a classic last-minute essay crisis. Interestingly, company executives usually do exactly the same thing, so the pattern of work in most modern pressurized businesses looks like this:

This last-minute approach leads to rushed and usually below standard work. Instead, businesses should do the hard thinking upfront and so create the conditions for a smooth run to execution or a launch deadline, like this:

Most people agree with the principle of this, but protest that there is so much work coming in that they can't keep on top of it all. A few people claim that they intentionally work this way because they work better under pressure, but the evidence rarely verifies this. So the beleaguered modern executive feels that their workflow looks like this:

Removing what little preparation time there might be in this relentless cycle, the net result for many is this:

And it never stops. There are three main strategies that can break this cycle:

1. **Upfront thinking built in.** Make it mandatory company policy to do proper thinking before all major projects or work cycles, whether annually, quarterly, monthly or even weekly.

2. **Think, then delegate.** As long as the right minds have thought properly at the beginning, then technical specialists and executors can get on and do the work once direction is set.

3. **Anticipate logjams.** A pragmatic overview of any run of work can usually predict when the trouble will occur. Doing this at the beginning and taking appropriate steps will reduce their severity or predict whether they will happen at all. This bringing forward of work is called precrastination.

THIS WORKS
Preparing early.

THIS DOESN'T
Leaving it to the last minute.

4. FOCUS
LIVELINES AND DEADLINES

As soon as a lot of talking and planning has been done on any project, somebody somewhere decrees a deadline. This is enough to strike fear into any executive because suddenly there is a tangible date by which everything has to be done. This places all the focus on the endgame.

However, this emphasis is more often than not misguided because it encourages everyone to concentrate on the looming deadline rather than the work that needs to be carried out beforehand. All this work before the deadline can be described as the liveline.

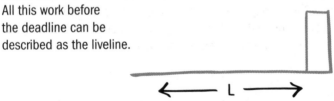

Deadlines typically take the form of a launch day or week, so they are almost always short, whereas livelines can be extremely long, sometimes years. This makes them far more diffuse and much harder to explain, so they need to be broken down into easily understandable component parts. One way to do this is to classify tasks by priority, as on the next page.

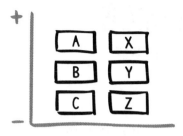

Another approach is to consider the level of energy needed to complete each element. Energy levels can be classified from **E**xtreme to **H**igh to **M**edium to **L**ow or **I**dle.

This interesting perspective allows company resources to be calibrated with required effort to create a realistic picture of whether tasks will be done on time or not.

THIS WORKS
Concentrating on live, current work.

THIS DOESN'T
Concentrating on the deadline.

5. PRECISION
FINDING NEMO

There is an old piece of wisdom that encourages people to concentrate on the doughnut rather than the hole. It sounds a bit trite, but we all know that much of what companies do is based on irrelevant distractions. So it takes sustained effort to focus on the really important stuff rather than the sideshow. When planning, how do we focus on the bit that really matters?

This is sometimes referred to as concentrating on the signal rather than the noise. One perspective on this is to work out the underlying reason for the work in the first place. In his book *Start With Why*, Simon Sinek's golden circle shows that most companies know what they do and how they do it, but not all know why. So the why must sit at the centre of all thinking:

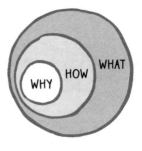

Once this is properly anchored, businesses need to get a grip on what they can truly affect. Too many executives are hooked on the past, but you can't change that. What you can change is the future, and now is where everything changes. This is what author Max McKeown calls *#Now* in his book of the same name. Between the past (P) on the left and the future (F) on the right, now (N) is where it all happens.

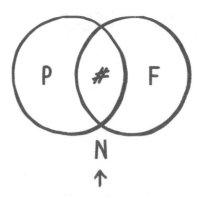

N
↑

As a final thought on planning, it is impossible to overstress the importance of truly knowing what you want to do. To make everything clear, you have to make clear decisions, which means cutting out everything that isn't essential. Imagine your challenge as a bullseye in the centre of an archery target.

In a NEMO approach, **N**othing **E**lse **M**atters except the **O** (the target).

THIS WORKS
Cutting out everything irrelevant.

THIS DOESN'T
Trying to do everything.

PLANNING SUMMARY

THIS WORKS
- Assuming the plan won't happen
- Anticipating work fluctuations
- Preparing early
- Concentrating on live, current work
- Cutting out everything irrelevant

THIS DOESN'T
- Assuming the plan will happen
- Assuming even effort across the year
- Leaving it to the last minute
- Concentrating on the deadline
- Trying to do everything

DRAW YOUR THOUGHTS HERE

A WORD ON WORKING

Most people have to work, and you would hope that most would like to get from A to B as efficiently as possible. But it doesn't always seem to happen that way.

Instead, people often go around the houses, waste huge amounts of time and may not even arrive anywhere helpful. So one of the most important thoughts when looking at how we work is first to decide what we are *not* going to do.

We then need to become adept at distinguishing between the destination and all the movement needed to reach it. Often people and projects veer off in all sorts of unintended, and usually unhelpful, directions.

We certainly need to think creatively to solve tricky problems and, contrary to much of what is said, we can be trained to be (more) creative.

Working in collaborative teams helps to get the best results, and so does removing ourselves from distracting technology.

Let's get down to some intelligent work.

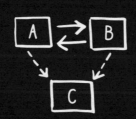

PART THREE

WORKING

1. PRINCIPLES
LET'S NOT DO THIS

Work is supposed to serve a purpose. Whatever the task is, it is intended to get us from A to B:

A ——————> B

The trouble is, there's so much going on in the average company that instead it often looks like this:

That means stacks of effort with little or sometimes no reward for it. So we need a more imaginative approach to working. We need something much more decisive and clinical. The key to this is working out what you do *not* want to do, or are *not* going to do.

The way to work this out is to write an anti list. Here's how you do it. Start with your list, and then work out everything that's on it that you do not want to do:

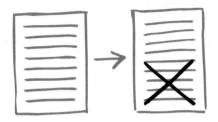

Now transfer all the stuff you aren't going to do onto an anti list. This new anti list becomes a statement of intent, a set of principles, a manifesto. Then use that as a set of standards. They are rules of engagement. You can do this as an individual if you have enough autonomy and authority, or you can make it standard practice for your department, or the entire company.

It's fantastically liberating, because now you can concentrate properly on what you really do want to do.

 THIS WORKS
Being clear about what you won't do.

 THIS DOESN'T
Accepting all work regardless.

2. PATHWAYS
DESTINATIONS AND MOVEMENT

When it comes to work, a lot of people are perfectionists. It sounds impressive, but it doesn't work. Perfectionists can't really define perfection, and they annoy everyone else either by micromanaging or by taking way too long to get work done. We need progress, not perfection. Naturally the work should still be of the highest possible standard – more like nine out of ten. Then move on.

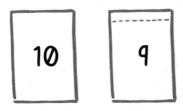

Don't confuse movement with progress. They are not the same thing. Lots of people, and indeed entire companies, generate lots of movement, but it doesn't necessarily mean they are getting anywhere. This could be because they are heading in many different directions without a clear view of where they really should be going, or because the path is ill-defined or not defined at all. Don't confuse direction with destination.

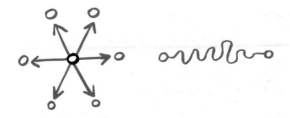

What is needed is action, not activity, and it needs to be the right sort of action. Doing lots of work may seem admirable, but not if it's the wrong sort of work. So we need a clear view of the specific type of action before we get on with it. And once we have done that, we will have less to do, but of higher quality.

The sum total of all of this is to concentrate on outcome, not output. In other words, it's not the amount of activity that matters – it's what happens as a result. There's nothing impressive about vast amounts of work for the sake of it, but it is impressive to reach a satisfactory outcome with the minimum amount of effort. That's intelligent work.

 THIS WORKS
Concentrating on appropriate action.

 THIS DOESN'T
Activity without knowing your destination.

3. CREATIVITY
MENTAL MAGPIES

If you want to be creative you need to be a mental magpie. That means constantly being on the lookout for interesting stimuli that can pique the imagination. These ideas then need to be attached to challenges to help address them and find an intelligent way through.

Some of this stimulation can come from reading widely, but there is a limit to what can be achieved at a desk, so you need to get out and observe and absorb.

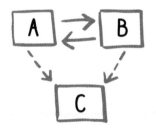

Ideas don't just jump out of nowhere. You need to start with a hypothesis about what might be an interesting direction. Then try to shoot it down by looking at the antithesis – the opposite of your first working idea. By analysing the tension between the two opposing views, you should be able to resolve them in a synthesis – merging the thinking or finding a middle way through.

This can take some time. Not everybody has an immediate 'aha' moment. It is important not to lose faith at this stage. The first step involves briefing your depth mind. Just because you haven't had blinding inspiration straightaway, it doesn't mean that your subconscious isn't working on it. We can use the metaphor of a submarine heading towards its destination. You can't see it, but it is getting there. So the conscious (C) is working at a surface level, but the subconscious (SC) is still working below that:

Despite what many claim, creativity can be taught. There are hundreds of idea generation techniques to choose from. For example, you can consider how a well-known expert or personality would approach the problem. Or you could steal an idea from a different category or industry. Or view the issue in a different light through the eyes of different types of people. Be relentlessly curious.*

* A full suite of idea generating techniques is available in *The Ideas Book*.

THIS WORKS
Being relentlessly curious.

THIS DOESN'T
Keeping your blinkers on and ignoring the world.

---

4. COLLABORATION
TEAMS AND SILOS

The word silo comes from the Greek *siros* meaning corn pit. Far too many companies allow, or even encourage, teams or departments to work in their own metaphorical pit, paying little attention to what goes on elsewhere. This is bad practice, and leads to disjointed decisions. Lack of teamwork in this respect has even led to the downfall of entire companies.

Cohesion and good strategic thinking emanate from productive cooperation between disciplines and people with different skills. So companies need to organize themselves accordingly, either forming multi-disciplinary teams, or setting up a hub and spoke system to ensure regular and powerful collaboration.

If these are not being designed from scratch, then a good place to start is to look at current working procedures and work out where things are flowing well and where there are blockages. Simply put, the work streams can be viewed as rivers and dams. Identify what is effective about the rivers and replicate their approach elsewhere. Analyse the blockages and work to solve them.

Interaction between teams works best when they pursue assertive listening. This is when someone makes their point clearly, and is then genuinely interested in what their colleague thinks in return. This can best be summarized by the sentence: "I have a view worth hearing, but I may be missing something." That's a genuine conversation instead of intersecting monologues.

THIS WORKS
Working together and listening properly.

THIS DOESN'T
Failing to cooperate with colleagues.

5. COMMUNICATION
TAMING TECHNOLOGY

One of the greatest barriers to effective work is email. It was once said that email is where wisdom goes to die. The worst examples of this are extremely long chains of emails in which the original point has been lost, and nobody can work out any more what should be happening as a result.

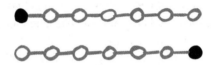

When requests and information move back and forth like this, it resembles a game of table tennis, in which the correspondence ping pongs back and forth.

This may be easy enough to keep track of if only two people are involved, but as soon as more voices are added, it's almost impossible to make sense of the conversation.

This becomes a cat's cradle that cannot be fathomed. One of the best ways to solve this is by adopting the philosophy of ping pong ring. In other words, if an A/B/A exchange has failed to resolve an issue or answer a question, pick up the phone. It cuts the email trail dead in its tracks and leads to enhanced interaction and better communication.

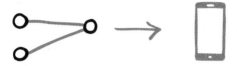

This simple idea could have much broader applications when it comes to taming technology. Most people are in thrall to their computers and phones. This leads to stress and even addiction. So if you want to interact really effectively with people, and communicate in the best way, there is no substitute for good old-fashioned talking. Phone is better than email. And in person is better than anything. How sad that this art now has a special name: face-to-face. If you really want to do your best work, remove yourself from your technology and think in peace.

THIS WORKS
Ignoring devices and talking to people.

THIS DOESN'T
Always using technology to communicate.

WORKING SUMMARY

THIS WORKS
- Being clear about what you won't do
- Concentrating on appropriate action
- Being relentlessly curious
- Working together and listening properly
- Ignoring devices and talking to people

THIS DOESN'T
- Accepting all work regardless
- Activity without knowing your destination
- Keeping your blinkers on and ignoring the world
- Failing to cooperate with colleagues
- Always using technology to communicate

DRAW YOUR THOUGHTS HERE

A WORD ON DOING

Given enough time, intelligent thinking is relatively easy.
Anyone can have an idea, but if it doesn't get done, then it
doesn't count. So thinking has to be followed by doing.

Doing is easier said than done. The first critical question
that everyone should ask is: what am I doing?
Without a decent answer, there's no point in proceeding.

But convincing ourselves that everything needs doing
inevitably leads to overload, so we need to develop
the ability to self-edit, get organized and only do
what will truly help.

Part of this is recognizing relevance – what is relevant here,
and what is not? All of us do far too much extraneous stuff.

So we need to become adept at assessing the true
potential of ideas, projects and tasks. And then ally
that skill with brutal and clinical decisions.

That means cutting a lot out, so the more decisions
we make, the less (unnecessary) stuff we have to do.
Keep checking: why am I doing this?

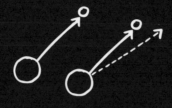

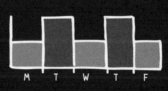

PART FOUR

DOING

1. INTENT
WHAT AM I DOING?

One of the most extraordinary things about modern business is the number of people and teams that start work when they don't actually know what they are trying to do. Usually this takes the form of a 'brief', but many requestors of tasks don't actually provide a brief.

The sentiment is: "I don't know what I want, but I'll know it when I see it." Anyone receiving such vague requests first needs to distinguish between a topic (on the left) and a thing (on the right).

A topic can be an entire project, whereas a thing is a specific, short moment in time – a thing to be done. Topics are qualitative tasks – they take time and careful attention. Things are quantitative. They are fast, and can neither be done well nor badly – they just need doing.

So we can assume that topics will take a fair chunk of time, whereas things can be done rapidly, usually in fast bursts, like the sequence on the left.

When it comes to topics, first we must establish that we truly know what we are doing – easier said than done in many companies. One way to do this is to use a briefing star to clarify five points.

WHY

WHAT — WHO

QUESTION   STATEMENT

Start with what: what are we trying to achieve? This must be bullshit-free so everyone is clear. Then answer the question why: why are we doing this? There must be a clear reason or commercial imperative. Then who: who has the ability to approve or reject our proposal? Name an individual so you know who your audience is.

The bottom two points of the star usually match the topic/thing distinction. The question is often qualitative and is a tricky, large issue to address: what are we trying to solve here? That's a topic. The statement is usually an objective – a quantitative task to do or a target to hit. That's a thing.

Thinking this way can help both individuals and teams. No one should ever start work unless they know what they are trying to do. Crucially, if the initial brief is vague, inaccurate or poorly thought through, then the whole project or task could well head off in the wrong direction.

If a rocket heading for another planet sets the correct course, then it will eventually arrive in the right place. But if the direction set at the beginning is a few degrees out, then the rocket will miss its target entirely. So it pays to be brutally precise at the outset.

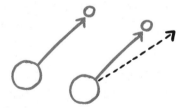

THIS WORKS
Asking: what am I doing?

THIS DOESN'T
Starting work without questioning.

2. EFFICIENCY
TASK TRIAGE

Most people have some sort of to do list, and what a mess they often are. If you are unlucky, your list is probably full, and may run to two columns or even two pages. If you don't have a system, it might look like the mess on the right.

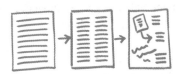

Many people tidy up and rewrite their list each day, usually at the end of the day or the beginning of the next. And almost every time, there is a residual pile of tasks at the bottom that hasn't been done, so the owner of the list transfers those tasks over to the new list. Then the next day, it happens again, with exactly the same tasks.

What is needed here is task triage. Triage nurses in hospitals decide the order of treatment of a large number of patients or casualties based on the severity of their injuries and the likelihood of their survival if treated fast enough. Your task list needs to be culled like this:

You can use all sorts of criteria to determine what should be on the list. It could be urgency, importance, financial opportunity, what motivates you most – anything. Whatever the screening process, these tasks need to be reduced, so that your list looks more like the one on the right, with just a few clear things to do today.

Now turn your attention to precisely what you are going to do to have a productive day. Quickly assess how long certain tasks will last. Five minutes? Fifteen minutes? Try to avoid anything being an hour or more and condense it into 45 minutes. Then map out your day.

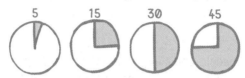

You can do this with your weeks as well, but if they always look like the week below, then you'll never keep it up.

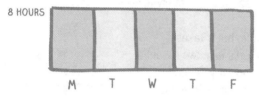

You need to plan thinking and planning times to pause, reflect and plan again. The week below still looks pretty packed, but at least there is some breathing space to catch up and recover.

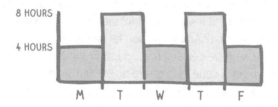

 THIS WORKS
Whittling down to a manageable number of tasks.

 THIS DOESN'T
Trying to do everything.

3. ATTENTION
RECOGNIZING RELEVANCE

Quite often people, and indeed whole companies, spend a lot of time doing stuff, but they don't entirely know why. Part of this is a willingness to please and seem diligent, but really it comes down to a failure to recognize relevance. In other words, is what we are doing here, or about to do, really relevant?

It sounds simple, but it takes concentration. Let's take two essential criteria: is it good for you and is it good for the company? If we plot that on a map, we should only do something if it is good for both.

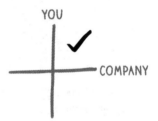

Everything follows from this. If it is only good for the individual, then are they being selfish? If it's only good for the company, then are the staff being exploited? And if it's good for neither, why bother? So let's assume we have decided that a topic or thing is a good idea, how do we get it done? Topics are bigger and slower, so step one is to work out how long it will take, and immediately enact the first step to get the ball rolling:

Things are short tasks that require a completely different approach. This is all about working through them rapidly and in quick succession.

Don't multitask, because it doesn't work. Don't have many things started. Start something, finish it, and then move on to the next, like this:

Don't mix up the two types of task. Block out proper runs of time for large topics, and short bursts for multiple things. For these smaller items, try having a 'think, do' session – probably about 30 minutes. Think of something, and then do it immediately. Repeat five to ten times.

Recognizing the relevance of these tasks has another dimension: don't do something unless you know why you are doing it. And on larger projects, don't forget the importance of momentum: you have to keep pushing it forward otherwise people will lose interest and veer off on to other things.

THIS WORKS
Looking at the relevance of your work.

THIS DOESN'T
Doing things in a haphazard way.

4. POTENTIAL
MAKING DECISIONS

In order to get things done, you have to be decisive. That means looking at a range of options, weighing up their potential and whittling them down to a small number of action points. It sounds easy, but you only have to look at the average status report or job sheet to know that there is far too much on the table everywhere.

The word 'decision' contains the Latin *scissus*, meaning to cut or divide. That's the same as in scissors.

So every time you make a decision, you cut something out, which means that there is less to do. Every time you do this, it improves the quality of what you actually end up doing.

There are lots of ways to approach decisiveness. First, try using a potential pyramid, starting with poor tasks, projects or ideas at the bottom, possible ones in the middle, and promising ones at the top.

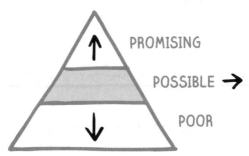

Remove the poor ones, and go again using a decision wedge, pushing the possible and promising ideas across into the probable and proceed sections.

PROMISING POSSIBLE PROCEED

Then use the judging triangle to verify that this topic or task is on brief, enactable and viable. If it isn't, start all over again. Two out of three won't do.

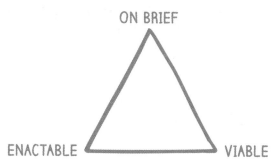

ON BRIEF

ENACTABLE

VIABLE

Assessing potential and making decisions is crucial to doing the right things. The process of cutting things out should never stop. It needs to become a way of life.

THIS WORKS
Recognizing potential and being decisive.

THIS DOESN'T
Assuming the best and doing it all.

5. PURPOSE
WHY AM I DOING THIS?

It's a question that many people have asked themselves repeatedly, and there's nothing more exasperating than a seemingly pointless task. It is important to understand the psychology of work so that we really can work out what we should be doing.

There's no better place to turn for advice on this than Dan Pink, author of *Drive*. According to him, there are three things that give a person motivation – autonomy, mastery and purpose.

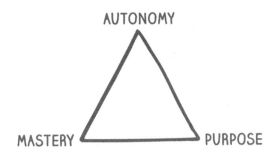

Autonomy means that you are left alone to get on with the job without being pestered. That's the opposite of infuriating micromanagement, and assumes that a suitable amount of time has been allocated to get the job done properly (quite unusual in modern business, it would seem).

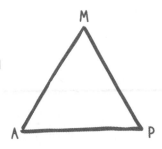

That would be great, but what if you don't have mastery over what you're doing? Mastery means both that you know what you are doing, and that you have the right resources to do it. This could be the right technology or equipment, or it could be a whole team – the manpower and womanpower to complete a complicated project. Without mastery, autonomy is a scary thing because you are left to get on with it, but you either don't know how to or don't have the right tools.

Which brings us to purpose. We all need it. This purpose could come from the very essence of what the company does, or from an inspirational CEO, team leader, boss or simply your own sense of purpose. Wherever it comes from, without it the work means less, or little or nothing.

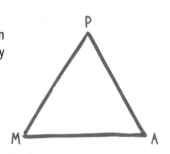

Assuming we can achieve this holy trinity, there is one other component that leads to great work – the concept of flow. People need to be able to get into flow to do their best work. So remove the distractions and let them get on with it. As all tennis and golf players know, performance is ability minus interference.

 THIS WORKS
Asking: why am I doing this?

 THIS DOESN'T
Struggling on without motivation.

DOING SUMMARY

THIS WORKS
- Asking: what am I doing?
- Whittling down to a manageable number of tasks
- Looking at the relevance of your work
- Recognizing potential and being decisive
- Asking: why am I doing this?

THIS DOESN'T
- Starting work without questioning
- Trying to do everything
- Doing things in a haphazard way
- Assuming the best and doing it all
- Struggling on without motivation

DRAW YOUR THOUGHTS HERE

A WORD ON PRIORITIZING

Putting things in an order of priority is harder than it sounds. Many bosses, and businesses generally, seem to want everything louder than everything else. As ever, part of the knack to setting appropriate priorities is to work out whether it is worth doing something at all.

Once that has been established, it takes courage and clear decision-making to trim out all the unnecessary stuff, so that everyone can truly concentrate on the things that really matter.

In fact, in any given moment, there should only ever be one priority, singular. More than one thing, and everyone gets confused. There are plenty of ways to sort the urgent from the important, and the good from the bad.

And then you'll need an uninterrupted run of time to get the job done, so fending off unwelcome interventions becomes a skill in its own right.

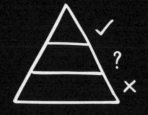

PART FIVE

PRIORITIZING

1. SEQUENCE
IS THIS WORTH IT?

We have spent some time looking at what needs to be done, and working out whether it really does need to be done or not. The next tricky task is to work out how much effort we should devote to it, and what should come first. This is all about worth, value and sequence.

Start by drawing up a pyramid of possibilities. The top section is stuff that absolutely needs to be done, with a high certainty of success based on past experience. The next level down has some

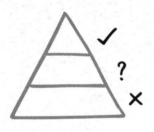

question marks – either we are not sure about the outcome, or perhaps we have never tried this before so we don't know for certain. The bottom level will probably not work, and, after investigation, should be removed from the work list.

The next stage is to conduct a thorough analysis of the questionable tasks. Are they really worth doing? Once you have done this, migrate any that, on reflection, look promising to the top section. Remove the rest and reject them.

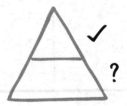

You will now be left with the very top of the pyramid – the capstone:

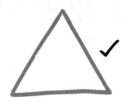

Now create a larger scale version of this, inserting the limited number of tasks with a high level of importance or chance of success. There should not be more than five of these. Juggle them around until you have them in the correct order of priority.

Then run a final check, asking once again of each one: is this task worth doing?

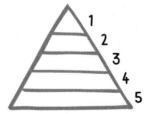

Now you have a cogent set of tasks, in the right sequence.

 THIS WORKS
Relegating low quality tasks.

 THIS DOESN'T
Not setting priority before starting.

---

2. CERTAINTY
ESSENTIALISM

It's not easy making decisions. As we established in the last part, to decide is to cut out and that takes discipline. This is what Greg McKeown, author of *Essentialism*, calls the disciplined pursuit of less. Most people have a non-essentialist approach, and it looks like this:

This mess needs migrating to something clear, as on the right:

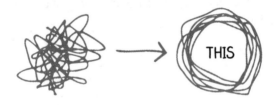

Now we have a clear sense of what to do, because we have eliminated everything else. This is particularly helpful when looking at time-bound tasks. You may have a lot on your plate, but for the moment (this morning, today, in the next hour), *THIS* is what you will concentrate on. Everything else can wait.

You can then look at the amount of energy needed to complete tasks, and balance that against how much you have. That could be you as an individual, or the combined effort of a whole team. Most people have too much on the go and, if they are non-essentialist, they will say yes to too much and end up with an approach like this, whether they like it or not.

Some people claim that this is skillful multitasking, but sadly it is now proven that multitasking doesn't work. Everything is started but not finished, there is a switching cost when moving between tasks and, for the final insult, those who claim to be the best at multitasking are in fact now proven to be the worst at it.

So we need to redress the balance by focusing energy like the diagram on the right.

Interestingly, the amount of energy used is the same – it's just dedicated clearly to one thing, and one thing only.

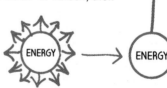

By pursuing an essentialist approach, we can move from "a millimetre of progress in a million directions" to "the one thing that will make a difference on this now or today." This also provides extremely helpful clarity for bosses and teams. If the boss decrees the one clear direction, and enacts it him- or herself, then the rest of the team also knows exactly what to do, rather than running around like headless chickens all day. It's good news all round.

THIS WORKS
Concentrating on one thing, now.

THIS DOESN'T
Trying to juggle everything at once.

---

3. SINGLEMINDEDNESS
PRIORITY, NOT PRIORITIES

When the word priority came into general use in the English language some time in the 15th century, it meant the very first or prior thing. It's from the Latin *prioritas*, meaning precedence or a state of being earlier. By the 20th century we had started talking about priorities, plural. This is where it all goes wrong. You can only have one. So by having many 'priorities', people are effectively operating on the basis of the Meatloaf song *Everything Louder Than Everything Else*.

This is of course an impossible state of affairs, so all these tasks need to be reined in and sorted out. One way to do this is to use a priority matrix, classifying tasks based on urgency and importance. If it's urgent and important, then clearly you do it now:

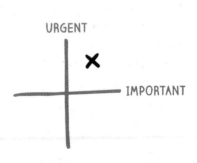

If it's important but not urgent (yet), then spend a short while working out how long it is going to take, and plan it in your diary now.

The knack here is to defend vigorously the time you have set aside to do this. Most peoples' diaries are obliterated by other people overlaying subsequent tasks and meetings later on. Resist this at all costs.

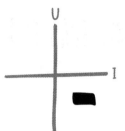

If it's urgent but not so important, then try everything you can to postpone it or delegate it. Remember that delegation doesn't have to involve you having people reporting to you. Often suppliers, other team members and different ways of dealing with a problem offer helpful alternatives.

And if it is neither urgent nor important, then you should seriously question whether it needs doing at all.

This way of organizing tasks allows you to set priority, rather than having a disorganized list with tasks dealt with in a random sequence.

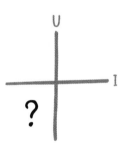

THIS WORKS
Having one priority, singular.

THIS DOESN'T
Having multiple priorities, plural.

4. IMPROVEMENT
GROWING PANES

Another way of looking at priority is by cross-referencing subjects by good/bad and old/new. This can be applied to ways of doing things, working practices, processes, systems – anything that a company or person does. The matrix takes the form of a window pane, like this:

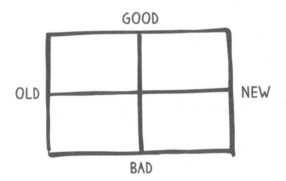

The vertical axis represents good at the top, and bad at the bottom. The horizontal axis represents old on the left, and new on the right. If something is old and good, then it goes in the top left quadrant, and so on.

If you have several practices in the 'good and old' segment, then that is fine. They have obviously stood the test of time, and do the job. If you have several of them in the 'good and new' section, even better. This means you are generating new ideas that really work. A blend of old and new is healthy.

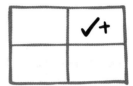

If there is anything in the 'new and bad' area, it needs careful analysis. It takes guts to reject an idea or process that has only recently been introduced, but surgery here is almost certainly necessary. Bear in mind that people are often very emotionally committed to new things, and will not want to admit that the project or idea should be dropped.

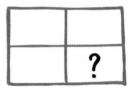

Anything in the 'old and bad' quadrant is clearly not working and should be dropped immediately.

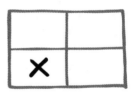

 THIS WORKS
Identifying good things without bias.

 THIS DOESN'T
Sticking with stuff that doesn't work well.

5. CONCENTRATION
BEATING INTERRUPTIONS

Being interrupted is the bane of anyone's work life. This is particularly true when the office is open plan. When you walk up the corridor, chances are you will be accosted by someone asking: "Have you got a minute?" Even if you are at your desk and clearly right in the middle of something, you will still be harassed. This kind of persistently interrupted day ends up looking like the bar code on a product:

That's a bar code day, and you can't get a run of time to get anything decent done. It's just too bitty. So the knack is to divide up time into suitable chunks, distinguishing between two types of work: quantitative and qualitative. Quantitative work can neither be done well nor badly – it's just stuff that needs to be churned through. Qualitative work requires more time and absolutely needs to be of high quality. Qualitative tasks look like this:

And quantitative tasks look like this:

So now you can plan your day or week in a new way based on the quantitative (QT) vs qualitative (QL) distinction. Start by allocating short bursts of quantitative time, in which you will knock over a lot of small tasks in one burst. Try not to do this more than three times a day, and never for longer than 30 minutes per session:

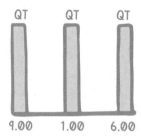

Then map out decent runs of time, usually a minimum of an hour, to do some proper thinking or creating. Interlock them with the quantitative bursts, and don't mix up the two types of work.

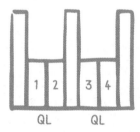

Review this blend based on your personal style, depending on whether you are a morning or evening person. Then apply it to a whole week or even a month.

THIS WORKS
Dividing up quantitative and qualitative tasks.

THIS DOESN'T
Mixing up quantitative and qualitative work.

PRIORITIZING SUMMARY

THIS WORKS
- Relegating low quality tasks
- Concentrating on one thing, now
- Having one priority, singular
- Identifying good things without bias
- Dividing up quantitative and qualitative tasks

THIS DOESN'T
- Not setting priority before starting
- Trying to juggle everything at once
- Having multiple priorities, plural
- Sticking with stuff that doesn't work well
- Mixing up quantitative and qualitative work

DRAW YOUR THOUGHTS HERE

A WORD ON PRESENTING

Presenting has never been easy. Sometimes the audience might be engaged at the beginning and the end, but much of the material probably won't be remembered. Being aware of the pacing of a presentation is therefore crucial.

It is vital to start strongly with something that really grabs their attention.

Then, do not dive in with your recommendation. Start by explaining what you looked into and how you developed your line of argument. This is the story of your investigative journey.

To avoid disappointment in the form of significant objection to your proposal, first identify what barriers might prevent the audience agreeing with you, then work out how to address those points.

Also, think carefully about how brave they want your proposals to be - simply asking them this before you create the presentation can make all the difference.

Following some basic rules can make presenting a lot less scary, and can hugely reduce preparation time.

PART SIX

PRESENTING

1. CADENCE
THE HAMMOCK AND BED OF NAILS

It doesn't matter how long a presentation lasts, it always follows
the same pattern, which is like this:

Research shows that people remember 70% of what you say at
the beginning, 100% of what you say at the end, and only 20% of
what was in the middle. This remains true regardless of how long
the presentation is.

In the middle is what has become known as the bed of nails. This
is the section you need to get out of as fast as possible, because
it's usually boring and convoluted.

So your main approach when preparing to present should be to concentrate on:

1. A really strong start.
2. A memorable finish.
3. A tight, cogent middle section.

In the next section we will look at how to start strongly (go for a grabber), and then we will move on to explaining your thinking (show your workings). But first you need a punchy start, a disciplined middle and a memorable parting shot, like this:

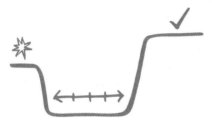

Also look back to part one section five to show how a well explained market map can help win the day.

 THIS WORKS
Strong start, disciplined middle, memorable finish.

 THIS DOESN'T
Rambling on in an unstructured way.

2. IMPACT
GO FOR A GRABBER

Going for a grabber means grabbing your audience's attention straightaway, and that usually means you need to say or show something unexpected or remarkable. You are looking for a controversial statement, a quotation that sums up the dilemma, an unexpected piece of data, or possibly even stating the opposite view to what they expect you to recommend.

One way to do this is with a number guessing game. Make your first chart a number, and ask the audience what it refers to. They will be engaged immediately.

3M

What is the 3 million? The budget? The number of extra potential customers? The conversation is now underway. Or try a controversial statement, such as: "This market is dead." The audience will probably be shocked. At which point you ask: "Or is it?" Then start to explain your thinking.

??

You should also choose an accurate and engaging title. *Presentation to Dave Smith, April 22nd* doesn't have any oomph to it. If you are starting a debate, choose a provocative question such as: *Why is our product so much worse than the competition?*

If you are trying to persuade them of a particular stance, then state it loud and clear: *Ethical Credentials: An essential element of our product positioning.*

If your purpose is information, keep it factual and free of loaded words: *The Banking Industry Today.*

If you want to generate emotion, put it in before the subject matter: *Touching People's Lives: The power of humour in customer service.*

Play around with the chosen title and constantly check it against the relevance of the content as it develops, changing it if necessary as you go along. Whatever you do, do not select an image from a photo library and use that as your start point.

THIS WORKS
Grabbing attention right from the start.

THIS DOESN'T
Slow, monotonous, even delivery from the off.

3. EXPLANATION
SHOW YOUR WORKINGS

To get people to agree with what you are proposing, you have to explain your workings. It's like solving an equation in a maths exam. You can't just go straight to the answer – you need to explain how you got there. The cadence of a presentation should involve whittling down information and options to arrive at a recommendation, like this:

This approach solves two major criticisms of most presentations. On the left, too many options are presented, so the audience either doesn't know what to choose, or just concludes that the presenter doesn't actually have a clear view. On the right, if the presenter goes straight to a proposed solution, the audience may only think they have the one idea, or that they haven't looked at all the options properly, or that they are just plain stubborn.

So the presentation requires a broad-ranging beginning, a logical argument in the middle, and a clear recommendation at the end. The knack with the middle section is to provide an intelligent interplay between assertions and facts. Assertions (A) on their own, without backup, can be dismissed or simply disagreed with by the audience, like this:

Equally, facts (F) on their own are dull, and don't get you anywhere without a point of view:

So the ideal blend is a series of assertions coupled to evidence (facts), or if you prefer, a series of facts linked to your point of view (POV) on what to do as a result, like this:

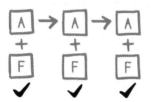

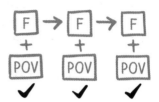

In this way, you guide the audience to your big reveal – the 'ta-da!' moment.

All sounds well, but beware the pitfalls of the big reveal here. Often in presentations, this moment isn't as dramatic as the presenter wants, so the knack is then to move swiftly on to explain how fertile the idea is. The shape of the presentation now looks like a bow tie. Condense down, explain your thinking, recommend and then expand out again to demonstrate how well the proposal will work.

THIS WORKS
Whittling down, proposing, then expanding.

THIS DOESN'T
Assertions without facts, or vice versa.

4. BARRIERS
OVERCOMING OBJECTIONS

No presentation ever runs completely smoothly. There are always comments, interruptions and observations on the way. But sometimes there are serious barriers. Often called barriers to purchase, these are severe blockages that, if not dealt with, will mean that the audience does not agree with the presenter, resulting in their proposal not being approved.

The way to deal with this is to think about it before you present. It sounds pessimistic, but the thing to do is to pretend that you are the audience, and write down all the reasons why they will reject what you are saying. These are the barriers. View them as a series of obstacles to the success of your proposal.

There may be one huge barrier like this:

Or two or three like this:

Or a series of much smaller points to address:

They all prevent the outcome you want. So, first identify them, and then work out how to build a case to prove your point, or disprove the barriers. Build these carefully into your presentation. If you attend to these points diligently, you should be able to knock down each reservation or barrier as you go along, helping you to arrive at a positive conclusion.

A word of warning on big barriers though: you can't rush knocking them down. For example, if someone has an entrenched position on a particular topic, you won't get them to change their mind on the spot, especially in the presence of colleagues. The more complex the argument, the more time they will need to come round to your point of view.

THIS WORKS
Identifying barriers and addressing them.

THIS DOESN'T
Assuming your audience will agree with you.

5. BRAVERY
A CRITICAL QUESTION

One of the great dilemmas when presenting is how brave to be. Some audiences are inherently conservative, whereas others want wild ideas. How do you work out where to pitch it?

One way to do it is to use a bravery scale, prompted by a crucial question that you ask the people you are presenting to before you even design the presentation. You ask them: "How brave would you like our proposals to be?" It sounds like a simple question, but the responses can tell you a lot.

Let's start at the conservative end. If the person receiving your proposal says, "5 out of 10," then you can produce reasonably safe suggestions, and don't scare them with whacky stuff.

If they choose 7/8/9/10 out of 10, then you have permission to propose adventurous material with their blessing.

If the answer is unclear, and you have the time and resources, you can offer a range of proposals with different degrees of bravery, such as a 5, a 7 and an 8.

Another thing to do is to calibrate the score they give you with the nature of the company they work for. If the company is inherently conservative, then their 9 out of 10 might be more of a 5 out of 10 elsewhere, and you can aim off for this.

You should also verify what their version of a score really means by asking what they believe an '8 out of 10' example is. This gives you a benchmark for their scoring system.

And finally, there are always some gung-ho customers who claim they want an 11 out of 10. These people are usually exaggerating, so be careful what you present. A range is probably advisable here.

THIS WORKS
Asking about bravery levels before presenting.

THIS DOESN'T
Guessing how brave they want you to be.

PRESENTING SUMMARY

THIS WORKS
- Strong start, disciplined middle, memorable finish
- Grabbing attention right from the start
- Whittling down, proposing, then expanding
- Identifying barriers and addressing them
- Asking about bravery levels before presenting

THIS DOESN'T
- Rambling on in an unstructured way
- Slow, monotonous, even delivery from the off
- Assertions without facts, or vice versa
- Assuming your audience will agree with you
- Guessing how brave they want you to be

DRAW YOUR THOUGHTS HERE

A WORD ON SELLING

A lot of people don't like selling, and they might not like being sold to either. But one way or another, we are all trying to sell something to someone, even if that's getting a friend to agree with us.

There is much to be learned from the way different types of people can be successful at selling, and surprisingly that includes introverts as well.

One big mistake when selling is trying to sell to everyone, or to too large an audience. Not everything is for everyone, so whittling down options for greater focus is advisable.

Nor does it necessarily pay to be relentlessly cheerful when selling a proposal – a dose of seriousness is often appropriate to reflect the difficulty of the task.

And there are plenty of techniques for structuring a persuasive line of argument – a good logic chain and some healthy involvement with the customer or client can also pay dividends.

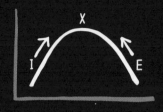

PART SEVEN

SELLING

1. CHARACTER
INTROVERTS, EXTRAVERTS, AMBIVERTS

Who sells most? Introverts or extraverts? Almost everyone answers this question by saying extraverts. So they would plot the graph something like this (I = introverts and E = extraverts):

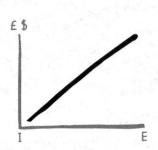

But fascinating data from Adam Grant at the University of Pennsylvania tells a different story. Extraversion is plotted on a scale of 1 to 7, so extreme introverts are far left and extreme extraverts far right.

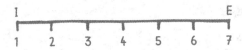

This is what the data shows:

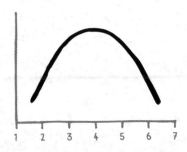

Perhaps not surprisingly, extreme introverts do have difficulty in selling effectively, presumably because they are shy in company, and possibly because they avoid selling if they can. Extreme extraverts have their own deficiencies, usually because they show destructive behaviour such as an excess of zeal and assertiveness, and a desire to contact customers too frequently. In other words, they pester and annoy people, and they don't listen well.

Those that succeed best are *ambiverts*. This is not a trendy new buzzword. It has been around since the 1920s and is designed to describe those who can find the balance between being 'geared to inspect' and 'geared to respond.' It's a powerful combination and hopefully of great interest to introverts the world over.

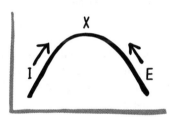

So the secret to successful selling is to find an appropriate blend of listening and proposing. Extraverts will do better if they tone things down and listen more. Introverts will do better if they can turn it up a bit, even for a brief period, because their listening skills will most likely lead them to a suitable and productive proposal.

 THIS WORKS
Being an ambivert.

 THIS DOESN'T
Being an extreme introvert or extravert.

2. PROSPECTS
THE SELLING PYRAMID

There are many ways to work out a sales strategy, and pyramids are one of the best. Starting with the basics, far too many companies try to sell to everybody. This desire for mass appeal fails to recognize that not everything is for everyone. So the first thing to work out is who understands your offer, who might do and who never will. Something like this:

You can sell with confidence to the top group. They are more likely to buy multiple times from you (frequency), they are more likely to be amenable to other products from you, and they may be prepared to pay a higher price.

Those in the middle section need careful examination. They might buy from you, but they might not. They need to better understand what you offer, and it's your job to communicate that. You need to work out how much effort and resource will be needed, and whether it is likely to yield an appropriate return on investment.

The bottom group usually represents too much work for too little return. The temptation is to keep trying to persuade them, but you are probably wasting your time and dissipating your effort.

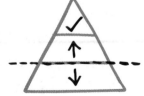

So the migration of customers from uninterested to interested can be plotted as a progression.

Then for a proper sales model, populate the segments with numbers:

You can of course invert the whole thing, with prospects filtering downward. This is often called a sales funnel, a hopper or a bucket.

The problem with buckets is that they sometimes spring a leak. One of the greatest problems for companies is when they attract plenty of new business into the top, whilst simultaneously losing existing customers:

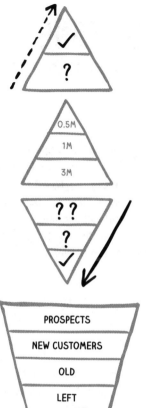

In a situation like this, retention and customer loyalty become more important issues than selling.

THIS WORKS
Categorizing sales prospects.

THIS DOESN'T
Trying to sell to everyone.

3. TONE
RATIONAL DROWNING

Some sales strategies and cultures rely on a relentlessly cheerful approach. But in many contexts this is counterproductive. In fact, it can pay to suggest that the issue is much harder than the potential customer believes. This involves taking the mood down for a short while to emphasise the severity of the problem, followed by bringing them back up with your proposed solution. This is called *rational drowning*.

Effective selling at the highest level involves commercial teaching, and it usually involves six main stages:

1. ***Warmer (W):*** build credibility through empathy. Listen, learn, emote and develop a rapport.

2. ***Reframe (RF):*** shock the customer with the unknown. Introduce something they don't know. Re-express the challenge in a new way.

3. ***Rational drowning (RD):*** intensify the problem, and then break it down into understandable components, using logic and data.

4. ***Emotional impact (EI):*** make the problem human. Give tangible and personal examples to dramatize the issue.

EI

5. ***Value proposition (VP):*** introduce a new approach, building confidence back up. This brings the prospect out of the 'drowning slump.'

VP

6. ***Implementation map (IM):*** explain how to fix the problem in detail with your product or service. Map it out so that next steps and indicators of progress are clear.

IM

Stick it all together and this adds up to a very convincing selling sequence.

THIS WORKS
Rational drowning.

THIS DOESN'T
Cheerfully saying the task is easy.

4. SYSTEM
THE TEN-STEP CASE

Selling effectively means you have to make a clear case. Here's how to make a case in ten steps.

1. There are various views (V) on this topic, which span broadly from V1 to V2 to V3. Let's take a new look at this.

2. The facts (F) are F1, F2 and F3.

3. We can shed a different light on this and investigate the issues in the following way (explain an analytical approach or method).

4. Analysing the whole picture leads us to territories (T) 1, 2 and 3.

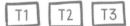

5. Of these, we believe solution T1 has the most potential.

6. Objections to this idea might include A, B and C, but they can be countered with data and evidence (E) 1, 2 and 3.

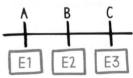

7. So, we recommend X.

8. X is a very fertile idea and can be developed in the following ways.

9. If enacted, the principal benefits of this will be excellent, a series of things ticked off effectively: √√√.

10. This line of argument can be summarized in a short chain of logic (L), which is $1 + 2 + 3 = X$.

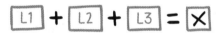

This approach is also perfect for structuring an executive summary of a sales pitch on one sheet of paper. In fact, it often pays to write this out *before* doing all the charts. Your line of argument will be more coherent.

THIS WORKS
Drawing up a tight logic chain.

THIS DOESN'T
Making up the case as you go along.

5. INVOLVEMENT
FOUR CORNER WALKABOUT

There is a way of selling without really selling. It is a technique that encourages the customer or client to invent the solution jointly with you. One of its greatest assets is that it is dynamic and inevitably leads to interesting departures, but is always completely anchored to the topic.

First, you need a room large enough to allow your participants to walk around. This may mean a big room, or you might want to rearrange the furniture or remove a boardroom table. Then take four large sheets of flip chart paper. Choose four pivotal thoughts about the topic, and write one only on each sheet. For example, if you are working on how to sell more cars, you might write down design, price, fuel economy and eco-friendly.

Place each sheet in a different corner of the room like this:

Give your first attendee a marker pen, send them to a corner and ask them to write the first thought they come up with next to the original word. They then move on to the next corner, and another attendee is sent to add to their thought.

Keep sending everyone round, each building on what has gone before until each sheet is full.

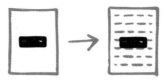

Then review the results on the four sheets and vote on the best ideas.

This technique achieves three things:

1. Lateral departures that are intrinsically linked to the topic (because the paper has a finite space).

2. Surprise and stimulation for the attendees when they see the ways in which their ideas can be built upon by others to generate something more powerful.

3. A sense of teamwork, in which the customer has participated in the solution, thus ensuring that they intrinsically agree with it.

 THIS WORKS
Coming up with the solution together.

 THIS DOESN'T
Failing to involve others in the decision.

SELLING SUMMARY

THIS WORKS
- Being an ambivert
- Categorizing sales prospects
- Rational drowning
- Drawing up a tight logic chain
- Coming up with the solution together

THIS DOESN'T
- Being an extreme introvert or extravert
- Trying to sell to everyone
- Cheerfully saying the task is easy
- Making up the case as you go along
- Failing to involve others in the decision

DRAW YOUR THOUGHTS HERE

A WORD ON NEGOTIATING

Negotiation can be nerve-wracking, but you can become much more effective at it if you study some techniques and prepare properly. It all starts by admitting that you are negotiating and then mapping out what's at stake on both sides.

You need to identify the variables and whittle them down to a manageable number of components, then work out their value to each party.

There are sequential steps that allow you to dictate the pace and, crucially, work out where you are in the process.

There are of course certain tricks as well. These don't necessarily have to be devious, and, in fact, a cooperative style almost always works better than an aggressive one.

As well as your personal style that you can choose before beginning, there are also important roles that you can agree with your colleagues before you go into battle.

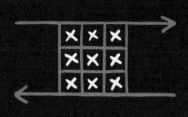

PART EIGHT

NEGOTIATING

1. VARIABLES
INTO THE ARENA

The Bargaining Arena is excellent for preparing for a negotiation. View yourself or your company as being on the left of the diagram, with the other person or company approaching the issue from the right. Like this:

The first point on the negotiation line is your 'must' limit (M) – the limit below which you simply cannot go. So, for example, if it is a financial negotiation and you are selling on a product or service that you have bought in for £7,000, then £7,000 is your bare minimum.

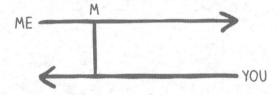

The next point is your 'intend' level (I) – the amount you intend to get. In this example this might be £9,000 to allow a sensible margin on the transaction. Your 'wish list' (W) includes any other benefits you would wish to have if the negotiation is going particularly well.

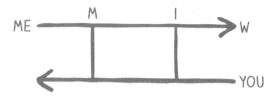

Plotting the other negotiator's likely must, intend and wish list points creates an overlap area in the centre. This is the Bargaining Arena, where a series of tradable negotiating variables can be identified and used to bargain with.

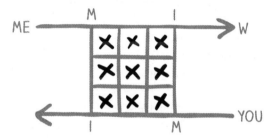

Bear in mind that what they want from the negotiation won't be the same as what you want, so trading these will allow both parties to come away satisfied. It's a form of to and fro, exchanging concessions, to arrive at an agreement.

THIS WORKS
Working out your must limit, intend level and wish list.

THIS DOESN'T
Failing to prepare or consider the other party's position.

2. OPTIONS
ONLY THREE THINGS

It sounds a bit crass, but negotiations only ever really involve three things: time, cost and some sort of quality component. So the IF Triangle is a crucial ally in any negotiation because it covers the only three variables that are ever at stake when a customer is considering whether to make a purchase. The three questions are always:

1. Will it do the job? (quality)
2. How much will it cost? (price)
3. When can I have it? (timing)

So we can draw that as a triangle like this:

When negotiating, there can always be some flexibility on any two of these variables, but never on all three. For example, the price can usually be reduced if more time is allowed. Quicker delivery may be possible for a premium price. And although no one will ever admit to wanting low quality, things can often be short-circuited.

It is called the IF Triangle because a good way to enact a successful negotiating stance is to start every sentence in the negotiation with the word *if*. It is impossible to finish a sentence that begins with *if* without attaching a condition – a crucial weapon in any successful negotiation.

Examples include: "If I have to deliver it by Friday, the price will have to increase," and "If you need the price to reduce, I will need longer to do the job."

As the sign in a shop once said: "We offer three kinds of services: good, cheap or fast. You can only pick two. Good and cheap won't be fast. Fast and good won't be cheap. Cheap and fast won't be good." Or as one client of mine put it: "The bitterness of low quality remains long after the sweetness of low price."

Another way to look at this is through a Venn diagram: fast, cheap and great. Fast and cheap will be hasty and careless (H&C), cheap and great inevitably takes too long (ITTL) and fast and great is a case of "You get what you pay for" (YGWYPF). The bit in the middle is an impossible utopia.

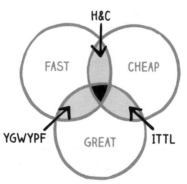

THIS WORKS
Working with the two out of three principle.

THIS DOESN'T
Putting too much pressure on all three variables.

3. PROCESS
EIGHT STEPS

Negotiation processes vary, but here is an eight-step approach that works well.

1. Prepare

Gather together all your lists and information, and agree your approach and roles, especially with any colleagues. Structure your argument and work out what concessions you are prepared to make. Write your list of issues, your realistic expectations and the minimum acceptable position against each. This enables you to frame up your must, intend and wish positions, as in the Bargaining Arena.

2. Argue

Contrary to what many think, an argument is not a flaming row. It is an opportunity to exchange information, review the issues, structure expectations and test assumptions. Here you should ask direct questions then shut up and listen to the answers, regularly summarizing what is being said.

3. Signal

Here the language changes from absolute to qualified statements. To advance the negotiation there must be a proposal. Look out for these signals, and reward them – don't punish them. Always reward signals with an acknowledgment, and use them to make progress towards a conclusion.

4. Propose

Propose, explain, summarize and invite a response. Never interrupt a proposal yourself. Consider your response carefully, and if necessary make a counter proposal repackaging the variables to suit. The idea is to give them what they want on your terms.

5. Package

Packaging adjusts the variables without increasing the offer in order to make the proposal more acceptable. Think creatively about these variables. Value your concessions in their terms – what are they worth to them?

6. Bargain

Bargaining is essentially a trading activity. For every component that you offer, always ask yourself: "What do I get in return?"

Give to get. Concede in areas of lesser importance to you so as to gain in more important ones. Always put a price on demands. The basic equation is: if you do X, then I can do Y.

7. Close

Eventually you have to bring everything to a head. Trial closing is a good way to flush out any remaining issues, something

along the lines of: "Are you saying that if I agree to both those items, you will be satisfied?"

8. Agree

Although it sounds as though closing would be the end of it, it is perfectly possible for people to walk away from a negotiation thinking that it is clear what has been agreed, when in fact it isn't. So you need to confirm what is agreed on the spot, for the avoidance of all doubt.

 THIS WORKS
Negotiating in clear steps.

 THIS DOESN'T
Letting things happen randomly.

4. TACTICS
NEVER SPLIT THE DIFFERENCE

Chris Voss is a former FBI negotiator. His book *Never Split The Difference* contains some principles that he believes lead to successful negotiation.

1. ***Be a mirror:*** repeat what the other person says to gain empathy, use silence to allow it to work, use a late night DJ voice to calm things down, and don't make assumptions. Mirroring is also called *isopraxism*.

2. ***Don't feel their pain, label it:*** use phrases such as "It seems like...", "It sounds like..." and "It looks like..." This creates empathy and shows that you have listened.

3. ***Beware yes and master no:*** no usually means something else, such as I am not yet ready to agree, you are making me uncomfortable, or I don't understand. Keep investigating when someone says no.

4. ***Trigger the two words that transform any negotiation:*** "That's right." That's the response you are looking for. You can build from there.

5. **Bend their reality:** make deadlines your ally, put the emphasis on fairness, anchor their emotions and establish a range of options.

6. **Create the illusion of control:** ask calibrated questions that start with "How" or "What."

7. **Guarantee execution:** you need the other person to say yes three times to guarantee that what you have agreed is indeed going to happen. There are three types of yes: counterfeit, confirmation and commitment.

8. **Bargain hard:** when you do talk numbers, use odd ones – it makes it sound as though they are properly calculated.

None of this is supposed to be devious. They are just important components of establishing trust and empathy.

THIS WORKS
Mirroring what the other person says.

THIS DOESN'T
Failing to create empathy.

5. APPROACH
STYLE GUIDE

At the heart of an effective negotiation style is tactical empathy – listening as a martial art, balancing emotional intelligence with active listening to get inside the mind of the other person. There are often many types of people in negotiations:

- **_Analyst:_** methodical, diligent, not in a rush.
  (time = preparation)
- **_Accommodator:_** takes time to build the relationship.
  (time = relationship)
- **_Assertive:_** getting it done is more important than getting it right.
  (time = money)

There are also various roles team members can play:

- **_Leader:_** conducts the negotiation, gives information, expresses opinions, makes proposals, trades concessions. They are not always the most senior person.
  (Their role is to _talk_.)

- **Summariser:** asks questions to test understanding, clarify and buy thinking time. They do not give personal opinions, information or concessions.
  (Their role is to *clarify*.)
- **Observer:** watches, listens, records and tries to understand the other party. Says nothing.
  (Their role is to *understand*.)

Some negotiators decide to adopt a competitive style: suspicious, intolerant, emotional, aggressive, pushy, threatening and devious. This is not recommended.

A cooperative style is better, which means being trusting, tolerant, emotionally uninvolved, friendly, diplomatic, open-minded, empathetic, flexible and likeable.*

When it comes to money, try using the Ackerman model. Set your target price. Make your first offer 65% of it. Make two to three more offers in stepped increments such as 75%/85%/95%.

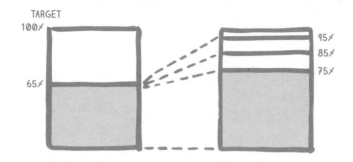

TARGET
100%
65%

95%
85%
75%

Use empathy and different ways of saying no in the meanwhile.
When calculating the final amount, use precise, non-round
figures. At the end, throw in a non-monetary item to show you are
at your limit.

Overall: use effective pauses, minimal encouragers such as *yes*,
okay, and *uh-huh*, mirror, label, paraphrase and summarize.

*If indeed it is possible for one individual to be this perfect.

 THIS WORKS
Choosing negotiating styles and roles.

 THIS DOESN'T
Making it up as you go along.

NEGOTIATING SUMMARY

THIS WORKS
- Working out your must limit, intend level and wish list
- Working with the two out of three principle
- Negotiating in clear steps
- Mirroring what the other person says
- Choosing negotiating styles and roles

THIS DOESN'T
- Failing to prepare or consider the other party's position
- Putting too much pressure on all three variables
- Letting things happen randomly
- Failing to create empathy
- Making it up as you go along

DRAW YOUR THOUGHTS HERE

A WORD ON PROGRESSING

Some people think that the main relationship in work is from the boss downward, but there's more to it than that. To progress, you need to manage upwards and sideways too. That requires significant emotional intelligence.

You also need an astute reading of interrelationships – an eye for working out how things fit together. That could be people, teams, departments and even whole companies.

Obviously if you are going to get on, you need to demonstrate the right skills and then have the confidence to make your case to gain promotion or a pay rise. That often involves a degree of emotional detachment, so you need to avoid self-deception and be able to see yourself in an unbiased way.

And you need to be consistent at work, so that you develop a reputation for reliability – a known entity that everyone can depend on.

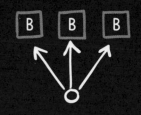

PART NINE

PROGRESSING

1. HIERARCHY
MANAGING: UP, DOWN, SIDEWAYS

Most people would like to be promoted, improve their standing and earn some more money. It takes a lot more than intelligence and the craft skills of a job to achieve this. Put simply, if an individual blunders around in a brash way and annoys everybody, then they are not going to get on. So progress also requires emotional intelligence. This is often called EQ to match IQ. Q = quotient.

$$EQ + IQ = PROGRESS$$

Assuming you have a reasonable blend of those two attributes, your career will progress. After starting out to impress their boss and succeeding, eventually someone gets promoted, and that usually means having someone report to them for the first time. This can be nerve-wracking, because people are often taught the craft skills of their job, but are not taught how to manage. So the first important skill to learn is managing downwards.

And you might have thought that, really, that was it for the rest of your working life – managing downwards, gaining more and more subordinates, and hopefully eventually becoming a leader (and there is no shortage of books on that subject – in fact, it is an entire industry in its own right). But actually there are other related skills that are just as important: managing upwards and managing sideways. Let's look at managing upwards first.

When you report to a boss, yes they manage you, but also you need to manage them. This involves telling them what you are up to, keeping them posted on developments, telling them when you want them involved (and when you don't), and involving them judiciously when things escalate. When you have more than one boss (B), you also have to merchandise your work list. That means explaining to all of them exactly how much work you have on, and what needs to take priority.

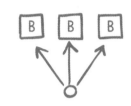

No individual boss will know the whole story, so it's your job to let them know all the time. So when a boss demands something immediately, you can explain that another boss has just done exactly the same. If they won't adjust their request, then get the two of them to sort it out because it's above your pay grade.

You also have to manage sideways. This means coercing colleagues into doing things that you need, even though technically you have no jurisdiction over them. That takes persuasion and charm, plus you need to reciprocate for them in order to keep the balance.

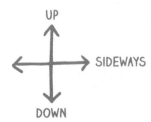

Many modern companies operate what is essentially a matrix organization. In such a set-up, many people have lots and lots of contacts working in different disciplines and sister companies, and they need their cooperation to get things done, but they have no true authority over them, so it takes a lot of skill to get everyone to respond effectively to your requests.

This becomes even more complicated when operating in a global network because many 'colleagues' in these networks don't even respond. Use any or all of the techniques in this part to manage relationships astutely.

THIS WORKS
Managing intelligently upwards and sideways.

THIS DOESN'T
Ignoring emotional intelligence and only managing downwards.

2. UNDERSTANDING
INTERRELATIONSHIPS

Overall, one of the greatest ways to progress in a company is through understanding. That's a broad word, so let's look at some of the components. The first thing to do is work out how the company works, which is often easier said than done. Start by looking at how the company is organized. This can be hard to fathom. Here's an example of one client's response when asked how they worked:

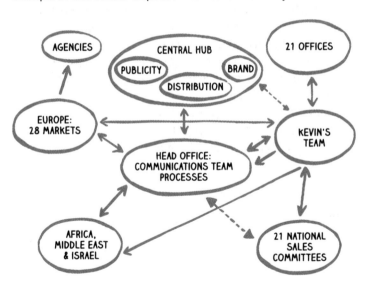

Hopefully understanding the interrelationships in your company isn't an impossible task, but it can be hard. So make sure you understand how the system works, even if it has flaws.

Then there is teamwork. To understand some of the tensions here, we can look to Patrick Lencioni, author of *The 5 Dysfunctions of a Team*. Have a look at what can ruin the effectiveness and cohesion of any team, particularly leadership teams.

Working up from the bottom of the pyramid:

- *Absence of trust (AOT):* this stems from an unwillingness to be vulnerable within the group. Those who are not open about mistakes and weaknesses make it impossible to build trust.
- *Fear of conflict (FOC):* teams that lack trust are incapable of engaging in unfiltered debate. This leads to artificial harmony.
- *Lack of commitment (LOC):* without airing their opinions openly, team members rarely buy in or commit to decisions, though they may feign it. So things remain ambiguous.
- *Avoidance of accountability (AOA):* without committing to a clear plan of action, even the most focused people fail to call their peers on counterproductive actions and behaviour. Standards fall as a result.
- *Inattention to results (ITR):* failure to hold one another accountable creates an environment where team members put their individual or departmental needs above those of the team. Status and ego take over.

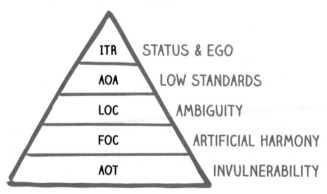

Lencioni believes three essential virtues make for the ideal team player (I):

- **Humble:** humility is the single greatest and most indispensable attribute.
- **Hungry:** these people are self-motivated and diligent.
- **Smart:** these people demonstrate common sense when dealing with others (it's not the same as intellectual smartness).

Those with just one quality are fairly easy to spot:
- **Humble only** = the pawn, who often gets left out.
- **Hungry only** = the bulldozer, who often annoys everyone else.
- **Smart only** = the charmer, with great social skills but low contribution.

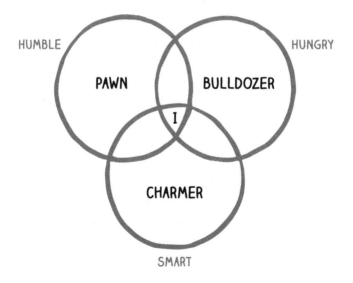

Those with two out of three are much harder to identify:

- **Humble and hungry** = the accidental mess-maker (AMM), unaware of their effect on people.
- **Humble and smart** = the loveable slacker (LS), only does as much as asked.
- **Hungry and smart** = the skillful politician (SP), out for their own benefit.

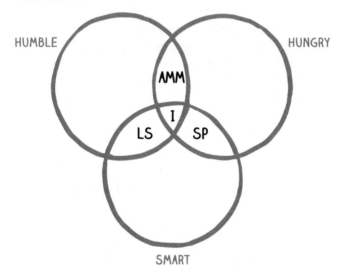

Understanding the interrelationships in your company, with your bosses and teams – that's the key to working out how to progress.

 THIS WORKS
Understanding interrelationships.

 THIS DOESN'T
Failing to navigate interrelationships.

3. PROMOTION
PAY RISE PLEASE

Some self-promotion is needed to gain promotion. It's quite rare for shrinking violets to get noticed. So you need to reconcile what your boss wants with what you want, or what you are prepared and equipped to do. Frequently this involves an inherent tension. It can also apply to customer or client demands on you.

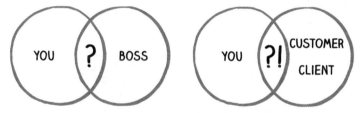

Crucial to this is the matter of self-confidence. Sometimes people have an over-inflated sense of how good they are. This is the difference between what you think you know (TK) and what you actually know (AK).

Meanwhile, others lack the confidence to make progress. If that's you, then you may struggle to see the gap between what you think you can do (TD) and what you could actually do if you put your mind to it (AD). The potential of the latter could be huge in relation to what you (currently) think you can do. See over page.

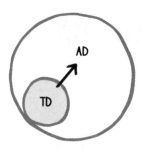

This can be based on someone's blend of knowledge and optimism. High knowledge with pessimism leads to stress. Low knowledge with pessimism leads to desperation. Low knowledge plus high optimism leads to conditional happiness. High knowledge and optimism lead to unconditional happiness.

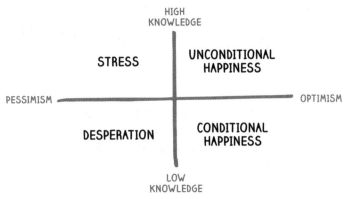

There is also an interesting distinction between know what I'm talking about (KWITA) and think I know what I'm talking about (TIKWITA). Someone who knows what they are talking about but thinks they don't will be overprepared but underconfident. Someone who neither thinks they know, nor does know, realizes that they need to learn. Someone who thinks they know when in fact they don't is prone to talk bullshit. Top right, it is a fine line between someone being a genuine authority on a topic or plain arrogance, depending on how they pitch the balance.

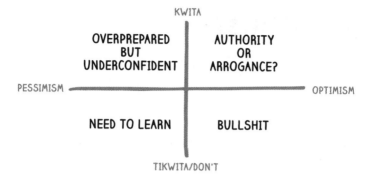

To succeed in earning a pay rise, a delicate balance of conveying these skills is needed, and it needs to be done in an unemotional way, with factual examples. Resistance to making progress like this can be summarized in what you could have, should have and would have done since your last appraisal. You need to overcome this resistance consistently to progress.

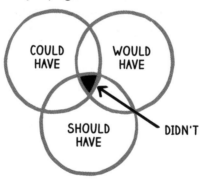

THIS WORKS
Maximising your potential.

THIS DOESN'T
Failing to take opportunities.

4. FEEDBACK
RADICAL CANDOUR

Giving and receiving feedback is a tricky business. Most people are familiar with the shit sandwich – a nasty middle section preceded and followed by something apparently nice. According to Kim Scott in her book *Radical Candor*, there is a better way to do it. Bosses can get what they want by saying what they mean – if they do it the right way.

Radical candour means you have to care personally and challenge directly. Challenging directly without caring personally is just obnoxious aggression. Caring personally without challenging creates ruinous empathy. Neither caring nor challenging leads to manipulative insincerity.

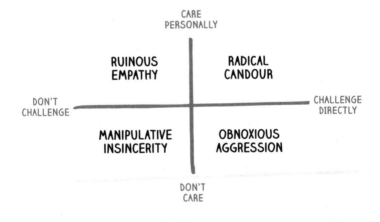

This matrix can be of benefit to both bosses and the person receiving the feedback – one for implementing, and the other to realize what the approach from the appraiser is.

Dawn Sillett, author of *The Feedback Book*, recommends the EDGE approach:

- **E**xplain: give a clear example of the behaviour that prompted the feedback.
- **D**escribe the effect of that behaviour, the impact on others.
- **G**ive them the microphone – invite them to speak.
- **E**nd positively with encouragement and commitment.

E	XPLAIN
D	ESCRIBE
G	IVE
E	ND

Often, feedback sessions end in an impasse because the two parties do not agree. This is usually because the appraiser finds that the person being appraised has an apparently inaccurate opinion of their own capabilities. In the eyes of many subordinates, they feel that they are grafting away and getting little return for it by way of recognition, financial reward or job satisfaction. Both parties would do well to discuss this blend and see if they can agree.

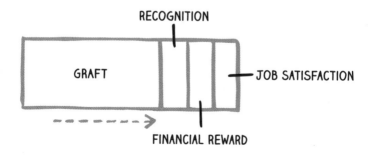

Such self-perception issues often arise when there is a gap between what the individual aspires to and what they are actually achieving. How far are they succeeding in their ascent of the pyramid? Both parties can discuss this and give feedback in both directions.

Sometimes, inability to achieve goals is caused by resistance (R). The question is: is it the individual who has built-in resistance to progress, or is something structural in the company set-up preventing progress? Both parties should review this and work out which it is, and then remove the barriers to progress.

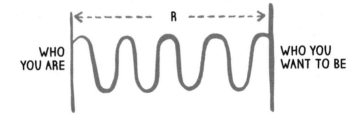

 THIS WORKS
Caring personally and challenging directly.

 THIS DOESN'T
Failing to discuss capability and aspirations.

5. CONSISTENCY
20-MILE MARCHES

Many people fail to progress in life because they lack consistency. In 1911, Norwegian explorer Roald Amundsen beat Captain Scott to the South Pole by consistently marching 20 miles a day. This was the distance that he had calculated was optimum for his men and their payloads. In bad weather he insisted his team did it anyway, and in good weather he stopped at 20 miles to save energy for the next day. Scott's team either stayed in their tents on bad weather days or overshot on good days and wore themselves out. Perhaps not surprisingly, Amundsen won the race.

Individuals should go for similar consistency, something that author Jim Collins calls 'fanatic discipline.' Start by pursuing consistent delivery to work in disciplined 20-mile marches like the top line, not the erratic bursts in the bottom one.

When you convert this into what specific individuals need to do, it helps to view each day as a hot date scenario, as suggested by Fergus O'Connell in his book *Simply Brilliant*. Most people's 'normal' working day looks like the line at the top of the next page – a well-intentioned day that then drags on too long. But what if you absolutely had to leave work at 6pm sharp to meet someone for a date? The mentality of this self-imposed deadline makes you a darn sight more efficient than if it were a normal day. The knack is to apply this discipline to every day.

NORMAL DAY | DATE DAY

9   6   8   9   6

That's at the personal level, but you can also suffer because your team is failing to deliver for you, and then it reflects badly on you. Kim Scott's *Get Stuff Done* wheel shows how to do it without telling people what to do in a dictatorial way:

- **Listen** (LI): give the quiet ones a voice.
- **Clarify** (C): create a safe space to nurture new ideas – they are fragile.
- **Debate** (DB): keep the conversation focused on ideas, not egos.
- **Decide** (DC): this is usually team consensus, not the job of the boss.
- **Persuade** (P): use emotion, logic and credibility.
- **Execute** (E): "keep the dirt under your fingernails" – leaders should not be above executing things.
- **Learn** (LE): openly – avoid being in denial if the outcome was unexpected.

Then repeat the whole process again.

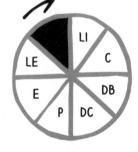

There are scores of other ways to increase efficiency. Try viewing your work as consisting of a few important things, and then a long tail of less important stuff. When you have decided where this point lies, chop off the tail or delegate the rest:

Try looking at all the working practices you have and deciding whether the old ways could be improved. Most of us have legacy habits that we should change. This approach involves breaking with the past – stop being wedded to old ways and invent new, better ones:

And finally, do remember that often small changes can have a big effect. As Archimedes said, "Give me a lever long enough and a fulcrum on which to place it, and I shall move the world." That's how you progress.

THIS WORKS
Having a disciplined approach to work.

THIS DOESN'T
Approaching work in a random fashion.

PROGRESSING SUMMARY

THIS WORKS
- Managing intelligently upwards and sideways
- Understanding interrelationships
- Maximising your potential
- Caring personally and challenging directly
- Having a disciplined approach to work

THIS DOESN'T
- Ignoring emotional intelligence and only managing downwards
- Failing to navigate interrelationships
- Failing to take opportunities
- Failing to discuss capability and aspirations
- Approaching work in a random fashion

DRAW YOUR THOUGHTS HERE

A WORD ON JOKING

We can have a lot of fun when we think visually.

If you are lucky like me, then people send in things
from all over the world.

Nothing is immune to a humorous perspective.

Pompous strategists in boardrooms are
a personal favourite.

The manner in which cultural characteristics can
alter views of time.

And the way various societal groups interact.

Time, causality, ethics and relationships
– it's all here.

Go on. Have a laugh.

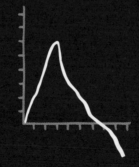

PART TEN

JOKING

1. **STRATEGY**
PARTHENONS AND ONIONS

Okay, now let's have some fun. After all the serious stuff about how to do intelligent work, let's look at how we can have a laugh with visual thinking. And there's no better place to start than with that old chestnut – strategy. Strategy thinking is a bastion of pomposity, with scores of companies trying to lord it over their clients with massive documents and presentations, most of them jam-packed with impenetrable diagrams. One of my favourites builds like this (imagine the narration by a very earnest presenter, with not a hint of irony): "Of course the foundations of the brand are blah, blah and blah..."

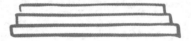

"The brand of course has four constituent pillars which are blah, blah, blah and blah..."

"And the overarching brand values are blah, blah, blah and blah..."

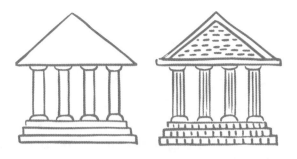

At this point no one seems to think it's odd or risible that a senior person being paid a fortune has drawn a fairly crap rendition of the Parthenon. Then, to add insult to injury, the whole thing is densely populated with scores of words – usually a ragbag of adjectives covering pretty much every part of the lexicon. This, apparently, holds the key to the success of the brand from this moment on.

But the skills here do not stop at a passing interest in Greek architectural styles. Oh no, it can be applied to pretty much any construct you like. Back to our windbag of a strategist: "THIS is the core of the brand..." (such a statement is usually accompanied by a reverential tap of the chart and a tugging of the metaphorical beard).

"But the content is so much more nuanced than that. Look for example at all the loyal user groups..."

"Now add the range of brand variants blah, blah and blah..."

"All encapsulated by our esteemed brand values – the glue, if you like, that holds the whole thing together. This, ladies and gentlemen, is our brand onion. It's a complicated construct with many layers and subtleties..."

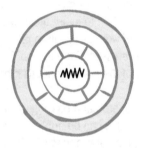

Actually, you can choose any shape you like, make it as complicated as you like, and populate the entire thing with as many adjectives as you can find. Fleets of marketing managers and advertising folk will then rush around reverentially for the next six months pointing to this as "the soul of the brand," but when pressed, no one really understands what to do with it. That is the power of a brand essence chart.

THIS WORKS
Stating what something is about in plain English.

THIS DOESN'T
Creating outlandish constructs that confuse everybody.

2. TIME
CULTURAL DIFFERENCES

Time is both a deadly serious thing and a hilarious one to map out visually. Here are some examples from *When Cultures Collide* by Richard Lewis – a serious academic work about how different cultures interact. According to Lewis, this is how a Spanish person starts the day and intends to schedule it.

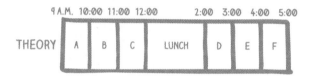

And this is how it actually turns out.

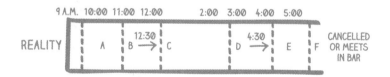

As you can see, the best intentions often get pushed back. Here is a Spaniard and a German discussing a deadline.

And this is what the Spaniard really thinks. The words they speak suggest a fixed deadline, but the Spaniard doesn't really see it that way.

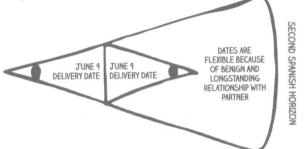

Here is how a Spaniard listens:

SPAIN LISTENING HABITS

And, again according to Lewis, here is how the French do it.

FRANCE LISTENING HABITS

Best of all, here is how the
Finns do it.*

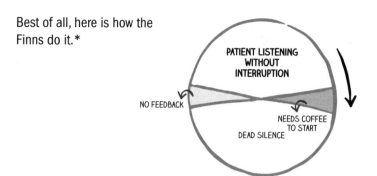

Here's an Old Finnish joke. How do you tell the difference between
a Finnish introvert and a Finnish extravert? The introvert stands
there saying nothing, staring at his toes. The extravert stands there
saying nothing, staring at the other guy's toes.

*To verify that Lewis's observations here are spot on, he was knighted by
the President of Finland in 1997.

THIS WORKS
Understanding different perspectives of time and attention.

THIS DOESN'T
Assuming everyone sees it your way.

3. CAUSALITY
ONE THING LEADS TO ANOTHER

One thing leads to another. Working out cause and effect is
vital to understand the world and avoid unwanted calamities.
Engineers have known this for years. If you want to fix something,
answer a few simple questions. The answer usually involves oil for
lubrication or tape to hold something together.

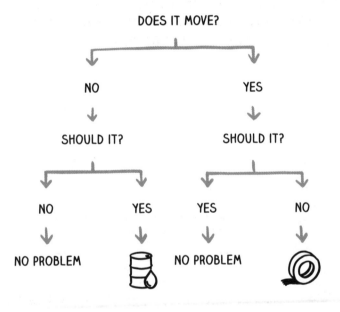

DOES IT MOVE?

NO   YES

SHOULD IT?   SHOULD IT?

NO   YES   YES   NO

NO PROBLEM   NO PROBLEM

You can take this scientific approach and apply it to almost anything in life and work. Does it work? Here's a problem solving flow chart:

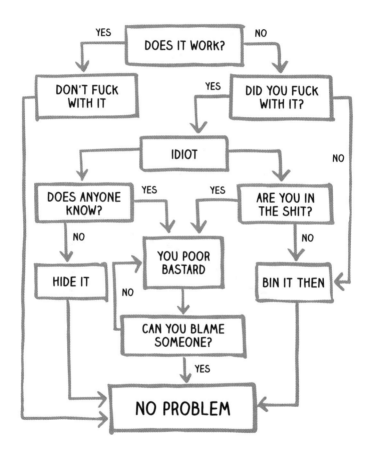

Once you get the hang of it, you can work out the relationship between almost any set of variables. Take for example the manner in which open-mindedness decreases as you grow older:

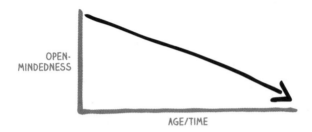

OPEN-
MINDEDNESS

AGE/TIME

Or how ego and vanity increase debt:

DEBT

EGO+VANITY

Yup. One thing certainly leads to another.

 THIS WORKS
Understanding cause and effect.

 THIS DOESN'T
Failing to spot causality.

4. SOCIETY
PREACHERS AND TEACHERS

Sometimes you just have to stand back and admire the quality.

This is my favourite humorous diagram of the decade. A Venn diagram can consist of just two circles, and sometimes three. But to combine four and cover such a diverse span of society is genius. What can we learn from bank robbers, DJs, preachers and our mothers?

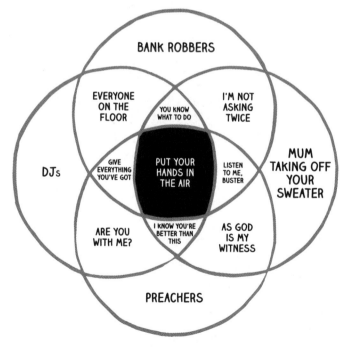

Enough said: put your hands in the air.

And while we are on the subject of society:

NEW POLL: IS SOCIETY DIVIDED?

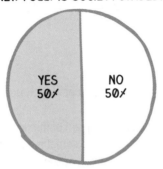

YES
50%

NO
50%

Of course, not everything in life is that clear-cut:

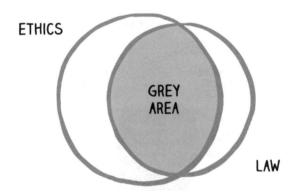

ETHICS

GREY
AREA

LAW

 THIS WORKS
Looking at society visually.

 THIS DOESN'T
Not questioning how things are.

5. RELATIONSHIPS
YOU AND YOUR LIFE

Two simple lines in all sorts of combinations can explain your closeness to those in your life. Let's start with your best friend(s) from childhood, or later at college:

CHILDHOOD

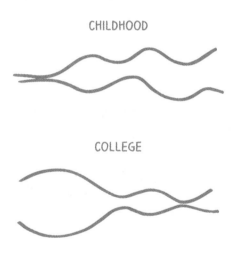

COLLEGE

Then we have the relationship with your brother or sister:

And of course, your parents:

There's your first love...

...someone you meet at the wrong time, then meet again later at the right time...

...the one night stand...

...and after all this you may well need a therapist, and you will have a relationship with them too:

And to finish, this graph sums up the attitude of most people as they grow older:

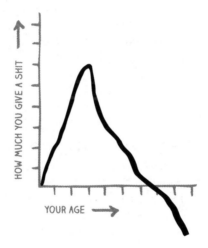

HOW MUCH YOU GIVE A SHIT

YOUR AGE ➡

THIS WORKS
Mapping life on a chart.

THIS DOESN'T
Failing to spot patterns in life.

JOKING SUMMARY

THIS WORKS
- Stating what something is about in plain English
- Understanding different perspectives of time and attention
- Understanding cause and effect
- Looking at society visually
- Mapping life on a chart

THIS DOESN'T
- Creating outlandish constructs that confuse everybody
- Assuming everyone sees it your way
- Failing to spot causality
- Not questioning how things are
- Failing to spot patterns in life

DRAW YOUR THOUGHTS HERE

REFERENCES AND FURTHER READING

Drive, Dan Pink (Canongate, 2009)

Essentialism, Greg McKeown (Virgin, 2014)

Great By Choice, Collins & Hansen (Random House, 2011)

Never Split The Difference, Chris Voss (Random House, 2016)

#Now, Max McKeown (Aurum, 2016)

Radical Candor, Kim Scott (Pan Macmillan, 2017)

Simply Brilliant, Fergus O'Connell (Pearson, 2001)

Start With Why, Simon Sinek (Portfolio Penguin, 2009)

The Feedback Book, Dawn Sillett (LID, 2016)

The 5 Dysfunctions Of A Team, Patrick Lencioni (Jossey-Bass, 2002)

The Ideal Team Player, Patrick Lencioni (Jossey-Bass, 2016)

To Sell Is Human, Dan Pink (Canongate, 2012)

When Cultures Collide, Richard D. Lewis (Nicholas Brealey, 2013)

ACKNOWLEDGMENTS

Thanks to Dan Ariely, Jim Collins and Dave Trott for their comments and kind words of encouragement.

ABOUT THE AUTHOR

KEVIN DUNCAN is a business adviser, marketing expert, motivational speaker and author. After 20 years in advertising and direct marketing, he has spent the last 20 years as an independent troubleshooter, advising companies on how to change their businesses for the better.

CONTACT THE AUTHOR FOR ADVICE, TRAINING OR SPEAKING OPPORTUNITIES:

kevinduncanexpertadvice@gmail.com
@kevinduncan
expertadviceonline.com
theintelligentworkbook.com

ALSO BY THE AUTHOR:

- *Business Greatest Hits*
- *How to Run and Grow Your Own Business*
- *How to Tame Technology And Get Your Life Back*
- *Marketing Greatest Hits*
- *Marketing Greatest Hits Vol.2*
- *Revolution*
- *Run Your Own Business*
- *Small Business Survival*
- *So What?*
- *Start*
- *Start Your Own Business*
- *The Business Bullshit Book*
- *The Diagrams Book*
- *The Excellence Book*
- *The Ideas Book*
- *The Smart Strategy Book*
- *The Smart Thinking Book*
- *Tick Achieve*
- *What You Need to Know About Starting A Business*